George,

Thank you for looking after us so well. It was a great pleasure to be hosted by you. Hope to see you soon

Best,
Khalid bin Bandar

Glympton Park Estate

A History

View of the house from the park.

Glympton Park Estate
A History

Text:

John Martin Robinson

Photographs:

Mark Fiennes

Phillimore

1998

Published by
PHILLIMORE & CO. LTD.
Shopwyke Manor Barn, Chichester, West Sussex

ISBN 1 86077 077 0

Printed and bound in Great Britain by
LAWRENCE-ALLEN LTD.
Weston-super-Mare

CONTENTS

I — History of the Estate

Glympton originated as a farming settlement in a clearing on the edge of the Forest of Wychwood. A royal hunting ground, Wychwood was very popular with the Norman and Plantagenet kings after the Conquest. Henry I in the 12th century built a luxurious hunting lodge at Woodstock in an enclosed park (now Blenheim) and this was extended and embellished by Henry II. This royal residence became the focus of the whole area.

After the Norman Conquest, William I reserved a vast royal demesne for himself, partly economic, and partly for recreation. It included extensive areas of forest for hunting deer, of which the New Forest in Hampshire is the best known and today the best preserved example. Fallow deer are thought to have been first brought to England by the Romans. The fashion for hunting deer, however, was introduced by the Normans after 1066. At first the sport was reserved to the King and his immediate Court. The Plantagenet kings in the 12th century were especially fond of this recreation and developed a series of royal houses or hunting lodges in or near the royal forests. Henry I's Woodstock manor was one of the largest.

Woodstock had already been a place of royal resort before the Conquest. Aethelred II (979-1016) held a council at 'Woodstock in the land of the Mercians'. Domesday Book in 1086 records the King's demesne as incorporating a chain of forests, Woodstock, Cornbury and Wychwood across central Oxfordshire. Henry I visited Woodstock frequently, and a royal charter to Abingdon Abbey in 1110 referred to Woodstock as the 'favourite seat of his retirement and privacy'. He established Woodstock Park and enclosed it with a stone wall in the same year, and built a house within it.

His grandson, Henry II, also much favoured Woodstock and kept his mistress Rosamund Clifford in a little house known as 'Rosamund's Bower'. He added extensively to the royal residence, which was situated on a steep bank above the River Glyme, laid out extensive gardens and established a menagerie within the park. Woodstock remained a favourite royal rural retreat throughout the Middle Ages, where the King and Queen could escape from the formality of the Court for private relaxation and recreation. Several royal children were born at Woodstock, notably Edmund of Woodstock, the youngest son of Edward I (born 1301), and Edward the Black Prince (born 1330), the eldest son of Edward III.

The proximity of this favoured royal residence had an influence on the development of Glympton. Henry II in the late 12th century extended the boundaries of Wychwood Forest to include much of the parish of Glympton. The area has continued to be partly wooded into modern times, and the ownership of the manor by powerful families in the Middle Ages was the result of its closeness to royal Woodstock.

The place-name was first recorded in about 1050 when Aegelric of Glympton witnessed a charter. Glympton means settlement or hamlet on the Glyme (shining stream). By the time of Domesday Book (a comprehensive survey of his new Kingdom of England ordered by William in 1086 to serve as a basis for tax assessments) the farming settlement was already well-established and the land was cultivated by 26 men. It then formed part of the English land-holding of Geoffrey, Bishop of Coutances in Normandy. Geoffrey of Coutances was the King's Tenant in Chief. The Bishop's subtenant at Glympton was called William and he was probably the father or grandfather of Geoffrey de Clinton [i.e. Glympton] who was chamberlain to Henry I. Geoffrey de Clinton is first mentioned in 1110 and certainly held the manor as tenant in chief, himself, by 1122.

His early life is obscure. Sir William Dugdale (Garter King of Arms in the 17th century) described him in his *History of Warwickshire* as a 'Norman who doubtless had his first abode in England at Clinton (now vulgarly called Glinton) in Oxfordshire, and thence assumed his sirname'. There is no other evidence for Geoffrey's Norman descent, though he is known to have owned property in Normandy and is recorded as giving a mill there to the Abbey of Savigny. He presumably came to the attention of Henry I while the King was staying at Woodstock and owed his rise to this lucky introduction. The contemporary monkish historian Orderic Vitalis, in his *Ecclesiastical History* of England, included Geoffrey among 'men of ignoble stock whom Henry I lifted up from the dust and exalted above Earls and Barons'. He was the ancestor of a dynasty which has continued through female heiresses in England to the present day. The current and 23rd Baron Clinton is descended from Geoffrey's nephew Osbert de Clinton.

Geoffrey founded a priory at Kenilworth in Warwickshire. In 1122 he gave the rectory of Glympton to his new priory as part of its endowment. This provided the priory with a certain agricultural income from tithes and glebe, and gave the priors of Kenilworth the right ·to appoint the priest to Glympton church. The priory presented regularly till its dissolution by Henry VIII in the 16th century when the rectory was bought back from the Crown by the then Lord of the Manor. Glympton was only one of many manors held by Geoffrey later in his life and his principal estates, and those of his immediate descendants, were in Warwickshire.

Geoffrey's grandson, Henry de Clinton, gave or sold the manor of Glympton to William Brewer, King John's minister, in c.1202. On the death of William's son, another William, without issue in 1233 the property was divided among five sisters. Glympton was held by

The estate originated as a clearing on the edge of the Royal Forest of Wychwood.

Glympton: the Georgian south front.

William's widow for life and then passed to his sister Alice, wife of Reynold de Mohun. Glympton thereafter descended from Alice to her de Mohun children and grandchildren and was held by the de Mohun family throughout the 13th century. By the beginning of the 14th century it had passed to the St Johns who were probably the first lords of the manor to live there. Thomas St John who died in 1432 was succeeded by his granddaughter Clemence and her husband John Lydeard. But their great grandson Edmund Lydeard sold the property in 1547 to John Cupper, thus ending a chain of ownership by descent, albeit three times through the female line, stretching back to the reign of King John.

Most of the early medieval owners of Glympton also had manors elsewhere in the country and do not seem to have lived continuously at Glympton, though a manor house, on or near the present site, is recorded from the 14th century. It is likely that the first manor house was built by the St Johns after they entered into ownership. In the St John accounts for 1326 are recorded expenditure on repairs and alterations to the house, and this is the earliest written reference to it.

The village which grew up round the church always remained small. In 1279 a total of 30 tenants was recorded and in 1377 36 people paid the poll tax. But in 1428 only 10 households were recorded in the village, no doubt reflecting a decline of population after the Black Death.

The Cuppers bought Glympton partly as an investment. They owned it from 1547 to 1632. The first John Cupper died in 1580, and his wife then leased the house. From c.1585 to 1610 the estate was rented by Thomas Tesdale, a rich maltster from Abingdon and an enterprising farmer. His widow lived there for another six years after her husband's death, herself dying in 1616.

The alabaster tomb, created under the terms of her will, is a major feature of the interior of the church at Glympton. On his death Thomas Tesdale left £5,000 to Oxford University and this sum was used to found Pembroke College. Tesdale augmented his malt fortune by growing woad and raising cattle at Glympton. In 1632 John Cupper, great-grandson of the purchaser of the same name, sold Glympton to Sir John Sedley Bt for £5,386,[1] but he sold it in the following year to William Wheate whose descendants, latterly through the female line, owned the estate till 1944.

William Wheate, who bought the manor in 1633, was responsible for much of the present layout of Glympton. He enclosed part of the parish, creating the park and moving the village from its old site clustering round the church to its present position on the other side of the river to the south east. He was also an active farmer. There had already developed a marked emphasis on mixed arable crops at Glympton, which probably went back to the Tesdales' time; wheat, maslin, barley, peas and oats all being grown in the early 17th century. William Wheate took a personal interest in every detail of his farm crops and stock. He branched out into sheep farming which was then very profitable. He raised sheep for sale at Bicester and Woodstock, as well as for wool, and experimented with rearing early lambs. His main arable crops continued to be wheat and barley with some peas and vetches.

The meadow and pasture belonging to the manor had been enclosed in the Middle Ages and 16th century, but the arable was still mainly in open fields in the early 17th century. William Wheate embarked on further enclosures soon after buying the estate. He exchanged land with other owners to consolidate his own holding and at the same time extinguished the remaining common rights on it. He also removed the cottages near the church. As a result, all the land round the manor house was enclosed, and a new park formed along the River Glyme. He also carried out improvements elsewhere on his estate, and converted Glympton Heath to arable.

William Wheate was born in Coventry in 1594. He was a successful lawyer of the Middle Temple. At the Heralds' Visitation of Warwickshire in 1610 the Wheates recorded a descent through five generations and proved their right to arms. They had considerable property in Coventry itself and elsewhere in Warwickshire, and had served as mayors of Coventry in the 16th century. William Wheate married Elizabeth, eldest daughter of Thomas Stone, a London merchant. His purchase of Glympton and establishment of a dynasty was typical of social progression under the Tudors and Stuarts, whereby prosperous lawyers and merchants invested in land, received grants of arms and established themselves as landed gentry. Many English

[1] The original receipt is in the Glympton papers now belonging to Col. Barnett …
'13 June 1632
Rec^d then of Sr John Sedley Barronett the just sume of five thousand and three hundred pounds wth use according for it fvó our Ladie day last past at 8 and rent unto the date hereof to pay in full discharge for the Mann^r of Glympton and the corne growing thereown the day and year above written
By me John Cupper'

The park and Glyme from the garden.

The Victorian bay window on the south front.

Victorian stables built by G.H. Bennett in 1846.

landed families can trace their origins to similar ancestors in the reigns of Elizabeth I, James I and Charles I.

Though William Wheate himself was too old to be directly involved, his occupation and development of Glympton received a nasty jolt with the outbreak of the Civil War between King and Parliament in 1642. Oxfordshire was strongly Royalist, and Charles I established his war-time capital at Oxford (London being in the hands of Parliament). The Royal Family lodged at Christ Church and Merton. Glympton was occupied in turn by both Royalists and Parliamentarians. In 1646 the Royalists at Oxford requisitioned food and carts. Two years later in 1648, 50 parliamentarian soldiers were billeted in the village, whom the inhabitants had to feed at their own expense. Mrs. Wheate, who was on her own at the time, wrote to her husband to describe the visitation:

> We had many souldiers went by Friday last, as rouges as can be, sweare and curse like their father the devill, talked much, but durst doe little, so I ordered them in som measure.
> They that quartred with us were one Capt Allsope, a very rascall. I had 15, the parson 15 and the rest 5. I bid them be civill and ordely, if nott they should find that I would take some course.
> Ours soldiers lay most in straw, only 2 bide and thanked me when they went away.
> My folks say the Capt was ashamed to see me (a rouge).

In 1949 a hoard of early 17th-century coins, mainly with the heads of James I and Charles I, was found buried on the site of the new almshouses in the village. They must have been hidden to avoid falling into the hands of the soldiers. They are now on permanent loan to the Oxfordshire Museum. The Parliamentarians are also reputed to have stolen the church plate which was only retrieved by accident three hundred years later and returned to the church by Alan Good who bought it back and presented it.

William Wheate died in 1659 and was succeeded by his eldest son Thomas. The latter had married, the year before his father's death, Frances Jenkinson, daughter of Robert Jenkinson of Walcot near Charlbury in Oxfordshire. Her father was created a baronet by Charles II in 1661, soon after the Restoration when the King similarly rewarded many who had been royalist supporters in the Civil War. Sir Robert Jenkinson's wife was the daughter of Sir John Bankes of Corfe Castle and Kingston Lacy in Dorset, who was also a notable royalist. Dame Mary Bankes had been responsible for the heroic defence of Corfe Castle, holding out for six weeks in 1643 against a stronger parliamentary force. A descendant of the Jenkinson family, Thomas Jenkinson, became prime minister, and 1st Earl of Liverpool, in the early 19th century.

Thomas Wheate was High Sheriff of Oxfordshire in 1665. He had two children: a son, Thomas, and a daughter, Mary. Thomas, junior, was less than a year old when he inherited the estate on the death of his father in 1668 and his mother was left the house for her lifetime. She lived there till her death nearly forty years later in 1706; her son Thomas sharing the house with her, even after his marriage. His wife was Anne, daughter and co-heiress of George Sawbridge. He was the most distinguished of the Wheates, playing a prominent role in public life. He was Whig M.P. for Woodstock in the reigns of William III and Queen Anne and a strong supporter of Marlborough. He was also Keeper of the Stores and Ordnance, an important post during the Allied wars against Louis XIV. He was High Sheriff of Oxfordshire in 1696, and was created a baronet in the same year. In 1705 he took part in laying the foundation stone of Blenheim, a sign of his close association with the Whigs and Marlborough. A contemporary description of the ceremony survives:

> Seven gentlemen gave it a Stroke with a Hammer and threw down each of them a Guinea; Sir Tho Wheate was the first, Dr Bouchell the second; Mr Vanbrugge the third … The stone layed by Mr Vanbrugge was eight foot square, and upon it were these words inlaid in pewter: 'In memory of the battel of Blenheim, June 18, 1705. Anna Regina'.

He developed the quarry at Glympton, but his hope of selling the stone to the Office of Works for use in the construction of Vanbrugh's new Blenheim Palace was dashed when it proved too soft and not sufficiently frost-resistant. He also completed the enclosure of the estate in the 1680s and 1690s, the parson's glebe of 60 acres being the last area to be sorted out, in 1691. He died in 1721 leaving four children. He was succeeded as 2nd baronet by his

A marble 18th-century chimneypiece brought to Glympton by Alan Good.

eldest son, another Thomas, who was born in 1693 and married Mary, daughter and co-heiress of Thomas Gould of Oak End, Buckinghamshire. He, like his father before him, was M.P. for Woodstock. He died in 1746 leaving four daughters but no son. His younger brother George, a lawyer, succeeded to the baronetcy but not to the estate. In his will Sir Thomas bequeathed Glympton for life to his widow Dame Mary Wheate. She died in 1765, after which, under the terms of her own will, their daughters succeeded to the property, the baronet's reversionary interest in the estate being bought out with the proceeds of the sale of Gould property in Buckinghamshire. The two eldest daughters Sarah and Anne, who never married, lived jointly at Glympton till their deaths, in 1805 and 1807 respectively. Following Anne's death the estate was inherited by her nephew Francis Sackville Lloyd, who added the name Wheate to his own. He was only squire of Glympton for a short time, dying in 1812, the year he served as High Sheriff of Oxfordshire. The estate then was much smaller than today, only 368 acres. By his will, his widow was to have the property for life, after which it was to pass to a cousin, George Henry Barnett, the grandson of Sir George Wheate, 3rd Bt.

George Henry Barnett was born in 1780 and lived to be ninety-one. He was educated at Eton and was a banker in the firm of Barnett, Hoare & Co., which was later absorbed into Lloyd's Bank. He divided his time, after inheriting, between London and Glympton, spending his summers in Oxfordshire where he was a J.P. and D.L. for the county. His wife, Elizabeth Canning, was the first cousin of George Canning the statesman and sister of Stratford Canning (Viscount Stratford de Redcliffe) the diplomatist. George Henry Barnett

The west front showing the reconstructed Victorian wing and the Georgian house flanking the new entrance.

The porte-cochère with Tuscan columns designed by Philip Jebb.

Detail of the columns.

was the model of a conscientious Victorian landowner. He substantially altered and enlarged the house on inheriting, and farmed half the estate in hand under the efficient management of a series of farm bailiffs. The home farm remained largely arable, with barley the chief crop, and also wheat and oats, turnips and swedes. In 1849 he built a new school on the estate at his own expense with accommodation for 50 children. He also converted the village into a model Victorian establishment, building solid new cottages in the local limestone.

On his death in 1871, he was succeeded by his eldest surviving son Henry who had been born in 1815. Henry was educated at Eton and Christ Church, Oxford, and, as his father before him, worked in the family bank in Lombard Street. He also played a part in county affairs in Oxfordshire, being sometime M.P. for Woodstock, a J.P., and Colonel of the Oxfordshire Yeomanry. As with many landowners of his generation, he was an active churchman. He was a member of the House of Laymen for the province of Canterbury (the precursor of the General Synod). Almost his first act in inheriting the Glympton estate was to support the rector in commissioning the Oxford diocesan architect G.E. Street to restore the parish church in 1872. Like his father he continued to farm the estate as a predominantly arable enterprise, his income from the family bank helping to cushion the impact of agricultural depression in the 1870s and 1880s, when the grain from the newly opened prairies of America and Canada drastically undercut the prices of English farm produce. He enlarged the park to its present size, by taking in the fields to the north in the 1870s and 1880s, and continued his father's work improving the cottages in the village.

He died in 1883. His eldest son George had predeceased him and was unmarried, so he was succeeded by his second son Frank Henry, born in 1850. He, too, had been educated at Eton; and had served in the Royal Navy. He, like his father and grandfather before him, was a J.P. for Oxfordshire. On his death in 1907 Glympton was inherited by his eldest son, in turn, George Henry, who was squire of Glympton during most of the first half of the 20th century. He was killed in action serving with the 60th Rifles (The Kings Royal Rifle Corps) at Calais in 1941. Three years later his son and heir, Benjamin Barnett, sold Glympton to Alan Good, the proprietor of Brush Electrics at Loughborough in Leicestershire, a firm which had been established in the late 19th century (and, for instance, had installed the electric light system for The Duke of Norfolk at Arundel Castle in the 1890s) and which had become extremely profitable as a military supplier during the Second World War.

The terraced extension containing the Games Room and Swimming Pool on the east side.

Alan Good only lived at Glympton for nine years. But during that time he carried out many improvements both to the house and estate, remodelling the house, re-planting the garden, and building some new cottages, and a group of almshouses in the village, the latter in memory of his young daughter Yvonne who died aged fifteen. He also provided a new water supply for the estate and modernised and introduced electricity into the farmhouses and cottages.

Following his death aged 46 in 1953, the house and estate, then 1,250 acres, were sold to Garfield Weston who four years later sold it to Eric Towler. Eric Towler took a keen interest in the agricultural side of the property. He erected many new farm buildings and bought some adjoining land, increasing the estate to nearly 2,000 acres, by acquiring farms in the neighbouring parishes of Wootton and Steeple Barton.

In 1988 Glympton was sold to the Australian tycoon Alan Bond but his bankruptcy brought it back on to the market almost immediately. It was acquired for Prince Bandar bin Sultan bin Abdul Aziz in 1990. He has transformed the house and estate since that date, buying another 500 acres of land and various houses within the estate, including the old rectory and Ludwell, reconstructing the house, laying out new gardens, replanting the park, establishing an excellent pheasant shoot and improving the farm. The Glympton estate has not only doubled in size in this century but is also among the best managed properties in Oxfordshire.

New Swimming Pool.

II — *History of the House*

The old manor house, first recorded in 1326, was probably built by the St Johns after they came into possession of the estate in *c.*1300. No trace of it now survives, but there is no reason to doubt that it was on the same site as the present house. The close juxtaposition of church and manor house is typical of medieval settlements. It seems likely that the house was remodelled or rebuilt by the Cuppers in the 16th century. The old gatehouse had the arms of St John and Cupper carved on it, which suggests that it was built in the 16th century. There is a manuscript account by Richard Rawlinson (now in the Bodleian Library) in which he describes Glympton in *c.*1700. He saw the coats of arms 'over the gate-house leading into the Mannour-house of Glympton'. This is usually taken to be a reference to the South Lodge into the park, but it is much more likely to have been a gateway in front of the house, similar to the arrangement with all existing Elizabethan and Jacobean gatehouses—Charlecote in Warwickshire, Lanhydrock in Cornwall, or Tixall in Staffordshire, for instance. There are no known examples of Elizabethan or Jacobean gatehouses at the entrance to parks rather than fore-courts. The heraldry would date the gatehouse to the Cupper period. Rawlinson also noted that the windows of the house had heraldic stained glass with the Cupper arms which reinforces the argument that they rebuilt or substantially remodelled the house in the 16th century. In the 16th century the house itself formed the nucleus of a group of buildings

The Family Games Room.

Entrance Hall with trompe l'oeil *ashlar stonework.*

and yards forming a self-contained community. A detailed valuation in 1632 at the time of the sale by the Cuppers describes it as 'A faire house etc, with a Dove-howse, orchards and garden, Mawlt howse, Backsides, Elmeyarde, and pook [stack] yard'.

A sketch plan dating from *c.*1705 of the old house (among the Vanbrugh drawings in the Victoria and Albert Museum) shows the layout of the ground floor at that time. The main block comprised a single range, one room deep with projecting subsidiary ranges flanking an entrance court on the north side. This was closed by a wall with a central gate facing the church. This, too, suggests continuity from the medieval manor house which would have faced the church and village rather than south and east over the parkland like the present house. The old house, in other words, had the reverse orientation to the present one and its main front faced north.

It is probable that William Wheate altered the house after purchasing Glympton in 1633. The 1705 plan shows that a large square open-well staircase had been installed to the west of the hall, and such an arrangement cannot have predated the second quarter of the 17th century when such spacious staircases first began to be built in England. The varying thicknesses of the walls and the odd siting of chimneystacks, together with an attempt to create symmetrical façades out of the asymmetrical main block, shows that an older structure had been remodelled in an age which valued symmetry and balance. It is probable that the central hall, with its entrance at one end, survived from the medieval house, but that the large room to the west with a bay window was a 16th-century addition, while the east wing, staircase and south elevation were 17th-century.

It is likely that the central three rooms of the house, as it was in the 17th century, survive and form the shell of the existing main block, shorn of the east and west ends and sweepingly remodelled internally and externally. The rubble stone walling of the cellar under the drawing room and the principal roof structure with sturdy oak trusses probably date from the 17th century. They, however, are the only old fabric in the present house which has been substantially reconstructed on four occasions in the 1740s, 1840s, 1940s and 1990s.

Sir Thomas Wheate the first baronet, was a man with a substantial public position and aspirations to match. His connection with the Ordnance and with the Duke of Marlborough's great project at Blenheim brought him into contact with Sir John Vanbrugh (1664-1726), herald, architect, playwright and man of fashion. The Duke of Marlborough was Master of

Staircase Hall designed by Philip Jebb. The trophies of arms were arranged by Alberto Pinto.

Detail of Staircase Hall showing the lantern.

the Ordnance and employed Vanbrugh to design buildings for the Royal Arsenal at Woolwich, as well as the new mansion at Blenheim, intended as a mark of royal gratitude to the duke for his victories over Louis XIV. For Vanbrugh Blenheim provided a 'unique opportunity to build on an heroic scale, uninhibited by considerations of economy'. Sir Thomas Wheate was close to Marlborough not just as his Oxfordshire neighbour, but as Whig M.P. for Woodstock and Keeper of the Stores and Ordnance. It was not at all surprising, therefore, that he should have been involved in the Blenheim project and come to know Vanbrugh. He assisted at the laying of the foundation stone of the palace in 1705. He also hoped to supply a large quantity of stone from his quarry at Glympton for use in the construction of Blenheim. But this proved an immediate failure. After only a year, in 1706, Vanbrugh wrote: 'I just now hear a Report I am much alarm'd at, that all the Glimton Stone in the Building flys to pieces with the frost'. The rumour of the stone's failure soon got around and was exaggerated. At Oxford, the Jacobite Hearne noted with glee: 'Tis said that the stones with which they build the Duke of Marlborough's House at Woodstock are extremely bad and that they crack by the Frost; so that in all probability they must begin ye Foundation again. Tis look'd upon as a bad Omen.' This must have helped undermine any commercial potential of the Glympton quarry, and Glympton stone could not be used externally at Blenheim, or indeed elsewhere.

The Library (top) with dark panelling, and the Sitting Room, both decorated by Alberto Pinto.

Sir Thomas acquired designs from Vanbrugh for remodelling his own house at Glympton with a new south front in Vanbrugh's characteristic Baroque style. The designs for Glympton survive in the Victoria and Albert Museum, with segmental-headed windows, pediments to the end wings and a central feature culminating in an arcaded chimneystack. Vanbrugh's proposed façade was wider (13 bays) as well as more dramatic than the existing south elevation of the house. It was too ambitious, however, and was not carried out. Perhaps the failure of the stone sales for Blenheim meant that there was not the extra revenue to pay for such a project, as well as demonstrating that there was not a reliable source of local materials for refacing the house at Glympton.

Though Vanbrugh's scheme was not carried out, the house was remodelled at some stage in the 18th century, almost certainly by Sir Thomas Wheate the second baronet, between 1721 and his death in 1746, perhaps in the 1730s when the adjoining church is known to have been repaired. A map of Glympton parish in 1807 shows the house as an L-shape representing the present main block but without the entrance hall and central staircase hall which are known to have been added in the 1840s (and reconstructed in the 1990s). The seven-bay south front, with its well-proportioned windows and handsome architraves with keystones, is Georgian. The 18th-century reconstruction of the house involved its re-orientation, as well as regularisation and re-facing. The main entrance was moved to the south from the north, which now became the back. There was originally a central door on the south front, where the single-storeyed Victorian canted bay window is now.

There is tantalisingly sparse information for the appearance of the house in the Georgian period. No drawings or watercolour views seem to have survived. The only 18th-century description of Glympton that has come to light is an extract from Miss Alice Dighton's Diary printed in the *Wild Flower Magazine* in 1903 and quoted in Canon Herbert Barnett's *An Oxfordshire Manor* (1923). This dearth of information is all the more frustrating as Blenheim was already a popular destination for tourists in the 18th century. But Glympton, then as now, was secluded from public view in its sheltered valley. Miss Dighton's description is, therefore, worth quoting for its rarity value:

> Monday August ye 28th 1759. Set out in a chaise and post chaise with Mr and Mrs Hope for Oxfordshire, Breakfast with Mr Price at Wycombe, and dined at the White Hart at Wheatley, a very neat inn, things good, sweet, and clean. Got to Glympton to tea. 'Tis a good old Mansion, one side dull, but the other toward the Park cheerful. You command a fine slope down to a river and pretty bridge and cascade. Altogether looks prodigiously pretty. We stayed here a fortnight with Lady Wheat and daughters and went to see several places while there.

Immediately on inheriting the estate in 1846, George Henry Barnett embarked on a thorough-going remodelling and extension of the old house. *The Post Office Directory for Oxfordshire* in 1847 stated that the house 'is now being fitted up'. The work comprised moving the main entrance from the south to the west and the construction of a new entrance hall and porch on that side; the enlargement and remodelling of the main block and the addition of a large new service wing, outbuildings and stables to the North. Bath stone was used for the work, being more reliable and long-lasting than the friable local product. G.H. Barnett kept the existing Georgian character of the main block. A single-storeyed canted bay window was thrown out in the centre of the south front to replace the old front door, louvred shutters were hung at the upstairs windows and Victorian plate glass substituted for small Georgian panes in the ground floor sashes. It is possible that the balustraded parapet was added to the roofline at this date. The new office wing, and stables, to the north, were designed in an Italianate manner with wide, bracketed, overhanging eaves and shallow-pitched slate roofs.

The architect for G.H. Barnett's improvements is not known, but it may have been an Oxford architect like S.L. Seckham who was responsible for various mid-19th-century Italianate developments in North Oxford such as Park Town. The result was to give the exterior an up-to-date Italianate classical appearance; the new and picturesque office wing provided the degree of asymmetry admired by the Victorians even in classical buildings.

The interior of the house was also totally remodelled at this date; any vestige of Georgian or earlier work being swept away to create a series of large, plain, high-ceilinged rooms. All the detail was of a standardised character with painted deal four-panelled doors and simple plaster mouldings and cornices and plain marble fireplaces. The exact appearance of the Victorian rooms is not known, however, for only the exterior of the house is recorded in old photographs and sketches, and the interior was re-Georgianised in the 20th century.

The Drawing Room with carved panelling and plasterwork.

When Alan Good bought the estate in 1944 he had ambitious ideas for remodelling the house. The identification of Vanbrugh's design for Sir Thomas Wheate in the Victoria & Albert Museum encouraged him to consider carrying out those proposals. They were drawn to his attention by Lawrence Whistler, the glass engraver, artist and historian of Vanbrugh's architecture, whom Good had commissioned to engrave two glass goblets showing Glympton. Whistler later wrote:

> I drew his attention to the Vanbrugh drawings, and he now has the idea of reshaping the garden front exactly as Vanbrugh proposed it, except that he would substitute a real door for a sham one, and carry the flues forward from interior walls. Consultations with his architect Mr. Trenwith Wills have been going on with that aim in view. Were it accomplished, there would surely be no other example in history of a design by a great architect being first abandoned and forgotten, then discovered, identified and carried out—on the site originally intended—and after an oblivion of nearly two centuries and a half.

The existence of building licences, which severely restricted the amount of structural work which could be undertaken, and diverted scarce materials into rebuilding bombed housing and factories after the Second World War, prevented this scheme from being carried out. On one of his engraved goblets Whistler composed a little verse:

> Behold the house that Vanbrugh might have fashioned!
> Behold the house that will be Vanbrugh's yet.
> If architecture is again unrationed.
> And his design (but lately resurrected)
> Is carried out by one who will respect it -
> Which will be Good - And England in his debt.

It was not to be, and in 1948-49 Alan Good carried out a less sweeping reconstruction of the house, working within the limits set by building licences and rationing of building materials. He demolished the north end of the Victorian service wing, reducing its ground area by about a third. All the single-storeyed buildings there—brewery, dairy, mushroom store, and the like—were removed. These amputations produced a stock of second-hand stone (not affected by building licences) which was used to construct new garden terraces on the south side of the house. At the same time the Victorian shutters were removed, glazing bars restored to some of the windows and various blocked windows opened up. At a stroke, these comparatively simple alterations transformed the appearance of the main part of the house from a Victorian one back to a Georgian one.

The Garden Hall with Victorian statues of Anne Boleyn and Sir Walter Raleigh.

The Dining Room decorated by Alberto Pinto in the Elizabethan manner.

The interior of the main block was also re-Georgianised to the design of Trenwith Wills. Once again this had to be done economically to comply with the building restrictions. The Victorian four-panel doors in the main rooms were made to look like Georgian six-panel ones by inserting an extra horizontal style rail, though they were not altered upstairs. Eighteenth-century pattern cornices were added in fibrous plaster by Jackson's (who have preserved all their original moulds). Genuine 18th-century marble chimney-pieces from demolished London houses were acquired and installed in the reception rooms. The work, however, was perforce rather meagre and makeshift and lacked the quality of Trenwith Wills's pre-war work. No doubt, if Alan Good had lived longer, the remodelling would have been carried further in a more substantial manner and the Vanbrugh elevation added. But all further alterations were thwarted by his premature death in 1953 and the sale of the whole estate to Garfield Weston. The latter remodelled the Victorian staircase, during his short tenure, to make it look Georgian by substituting a new 18th-century S-pattern wrought-iron balustrade. Otherwise he, and the subsequent owner Eric Towler, made do with interior decoration and made few structural alterations to the building. Alan Bond, when he bought the estate, had ambitious plans but got no further than remodelling the lake in the park before he was forced to re-sell. It has, therefore, been left to the present owner to remodel and re-plan the house, though the listing of the building as being of special architectural or historic interest has reduced the scope for external alteration and prevented any consideration of carrying out Vanbrugh's design.

Guest Bedroom.

III — The House Today

A major aspect of the transformation of Glympton for Prince Bandar since the purchase of the estate has been the reconstruction of the house to form a large modern mansion. The accommodation has been doubled in size, but the work has been carried out in such a way as to maintain the previous character of the house, and not to unbalance the 18th-century view of the house in the park as seen from the south. The extra space has been gained by rebuilding the Victorian service wing, using the old materials and keeping to the 19th-century Italianate style, on a larger scale, and also by building a large projecting basement storey on the east side, the full scale of which is masked by the design of the garden terraces on that side. The main block has also been increased in size with a new entrance hall, full-height staircase hall and a large dining room all on a larger scale than the previous arrangements.

    The architect for the redesign of the house was Philip Jebb and the reconstruction of Glympton was his last work, as sadly he died of cancer before the house was completed. Philip Jebb was one of the most accomplished architects working in a traditional style in England in the post-war period. His practice consisted entirely of work to private houses, both restoration and reconstruction, and also new houses in a Georgian manner. His work is remarkably accomplished,

French mirror in a bathroom.

A bathroom.

self-effacing and intended to perpetuate the existing form of a building, but showing an assured grasp of the classical vocabulary and the handling of traditional forms and materials. Other major works by him included the restoration of Cornbury Park in Oxfordshire for Lord Rotherwick and Woolbeding in Sussex for Simon Sainsbury, and a new dower house at North Port on the Lennoxlove estate in East Lothian for Elizabeth, Duchess of Hamilton in 1978.

The intention at Glympton was not only to retain the exterior of the Georgian main block, with the elegant south façade, but also to demolish the Victorian part of the house and to rebuild it on a larger scale; and to reconstruct the interior. Glympton is a Grade II listed building, and consent was required both from the West Oxfordshire District Council and also English Heritage. Initial consultations with these two organisations in summer 1991 led to some modification of the original design. They accepted that the interior of the house was of limited interest, being plain Victorian and extensively altered in 1947-8, and that the truncated service wing had lost its original plan-form. They had no objection to the radical transformation of these aspects of the building, but they were keen to preserve the surviving 17th-century trusses in the roof of the south front, and also wished to keep the asymmetrical character of the west entrance front with its sharp juxtaposition of Georgian and Victorian which they thought illustrated the history of the development of the building. Philip Jebb had been keen to design a new symmetrical seven-bay frontage for the entrance side of the house with a central pediment, and his first proposals show this. But on receipt of the planners' views he redesigned this to meet their suggestions, widening the return elevation of the Georgian block from two bays to a more compatible three bays and designing the rest of the elevation in the

'Gardener's Cottage' extended by Philip Jebb.

1840s Italianate manner. A large porte-cochère was also added at the client's request and Philip Jebb turned this into a virtuoso display of the Tuscan order with columns and pediments.

The Oxford firm of Nicholas Johnston and Peter Cave were employed to work with Philip Jebb and to supervise the construction on site. The building contract was awarded to the specialist London firm Holloway White Allom, who had made their reputation for high quality work earlier this century in Mayfair. Building began on site in September 1992 and was completed in June 1996.

The part subterranean extensions on the east side involved excavation and the construction of new foundations and retaining walls, the foundations of which stand directly on the bed of the Glympton stone seam. This new part of the house contains an American racquet ball court, an indoor swimming pool and a comfortable Family Games Room opening into the garden through French windows. The Victorian service wing to the north was taken down and rebuilt in the same style but containing rooms on both sides of a central corridor. It houses the kitchens and staff accommodation. The large kitchen is at basement level. There is a smaller Warming Kitchen on the main floor adjacent to the Dining Room.

Philip Jebb successfully redesigned the entrance hall and staircase hall with more ample proportions than their Victorian predecessors. The entrance hall is now a cube, and the staircase hall rises the full height of the house with arcaded walls, domed ceiling and an elegant cantilevered stone staircase. The wrought-iron balustrade incorporates the S-pattern panels from the 1950s staircase. The staircase hall is the most complete of Philip Jebb's designs within the house. Elsewhere his hand is restricted to details like the subtle circular patterned stone floor of the entrance hall. Most of the interior was designed by the decorator Alberto Pinto. He was responsible for the simulated stone on the walls of the halls, and the ornamental trophies of arms inspired by 17th-century royal armouries, in the Staircase Hall.

The principal reception rooms along the south and east fronts are designed in a richly eclectic array of period styles by Alberto Pinto. The Library has carved pine panelling and fitted bookcases of 17th-century character. The Sitting Room has a Palladian flavour, with stencilled walls, pedimented doorcases and an 18th-century chimneypiece of Siena marble in the manner of Cheere. The Drawing Room is richly decorated in an Italianate manner. The Garden Hall owes its basic circular shape to Philip Jebb, and has walls painted with murals to look like tapestry according to a scheme devised by Alberto Pinto. Four Victorian statues of Tudor and Elizabethan figures stand round the room. They are Henry VIII, Anne Boleyn, Elizabeth I and Sir Walter Raleigh. This circular lobby acts as an ante room between the Staircase Hall axis and the garden, and between the Drawing Room and the Dining Room. The

South Lodge, a picturesque feature of the park.

latter was designed by Alberto Pinto in the Elizabethan manner with a geometrical ribbed plaster ceiling, oak panelling and an elaborate overmantel. The upholstery and hangings are blue and silver, and the chandeliers are silver, which forms a good foil to the dark oak of the walls and complements the rich display of plate when the room is in use.

On the first floor the principal bedrooms are divided into suites for family and guests with dressing rooms, sitting rooms, bedrooms and bathrooms. All the decoration in these rooms was designed by Alberto Pinto including the attractive tile work in the guest bathrooms. The bedrooms have good, brought-in 18th-century chimney-pieces. That now in the principal bedroom was acquired by Alan Good and was formerly in the library. It is probably Irish Georgian work with Bossi decoration and a fine large panel of blue john in the frieze where the natural grain of the fluorspar depicts a ram's head.

As well as the principal house, Philip Jebb also designed a number of subsidiary buildings which pay tribute to the style of the Victorian wing. These include the Gardener's Cottage, next to the walled garden which has been enlarged, and has overhanging Tuscan eaves and Gothick casement windows. The faithful extensions to South Lodge, for extra staff accommodation, and the reception building near the church are also examples of the Glympton estate style. Since Philip Jebb's death, Nicholas Johnston and Peter Cave have continued to design estate buildings in the same spirit and they were responsible for the South Lodge extensions. Current proposals include the reconstruction of Hill View on the north drive, and a thatched rustic pavilion with tree trunk verandah intended as an occasional retreat and eye-catcher under the chestnut trees on the east side of the lake.

IV — The Park

The park was formed in the 1630s and 1640s by William Wheate after his purchase of the manor, and subsequent removal of the village, exchanges, consolidation and enclosures of the land. The park must have been complete by 1655 when Wheate's son is described as being of 'Glympton <u>Park</u>'. By the mid-18th century the park had achieved its current character as an informal English landscape design. The River Glyme had already been dammed in the Middle Ages to form a fish pond, but the whole stretch through the park was widened in the 18th century to give the appearance of a sinuous lake. In 1759 Miss Dighton recorded that there was a bridge over it, now gone. The park was surrounded in the 18th century by continuous belts of broad-leaved trees, and clumps or individual specimens were dotted over the grassland to accentuate the contours and frame the views. The ha-ha south of the house, between the garden and park, probably also dates from the 18th century, but has been moved and extended in the 20th century. The walled kitchen garden was also formed in the 18th century; it is shown on Pratley's map of 1807. The north and south drives also existed on their present line by that time.

A certain mystery surrounds the South Lodge, once the main entrance and the principal architectural incident in the park. It was obviously designed as an eye-catcher as well as an entrance. It is generally assumed to be of 17th-century origin and to be the 'gatehouse' referred to by Richard Rawlinson in c.1707. But it is likely that the gatehouse seen by Rawlinson, with its heraldic decoration, was contiguous with the main house and not at the park entrance. South Lodge probably dates from c.1800. A lodge is certainly shown on this site on the 1807 map. It was altered and made more picturesque in 1880 and now looks a Victorian structure. It has recently been tactfully extended at either side in the same style to provide more accommodation.

In the 19th century Glympton was a well-known deer park. There may have been deer in the park from its creation in the 17th century. The earliest recorded mention of deer at Glympton, however, is in a will dated 1797. By 1867 there was a herd of 60 fallow deer in the park and by 1892 this had increased to 70; though not a large herd by Victorian standards, it was thought to include some of the best fallow deer in Oxfordshire. The increase in the size of the herd in the 19th century reflected the expansion in the acreage of the park. At the

The Temple, originally built in 1846 as a dairy.

The replanted terraces on the South Front.

New parterre designed by François Goffinet.

beginning of the century it was only 60 acres to the south of the house. By 1833 it had been extended to take in the east bank of the lake as far as the fosse or sunken footpath, and by 1867 it was 72 acres. It was further enlarged, to the north, in 1875 and in the 1880s, and by 1900 was over one hundred acres. Today the park comprises about one hundred and sixty acres.

The same process of enlargement, and alteration in detail, has occurred in the garden around the house. No traces of the 17th- and early 18th-century layout now remain. But the general form with the ha-ha on the south front dividing the lawn from the park, and the spacious walled garden west of the drive and church, survive from the Georgian period. In the 19th century, the garden round the house was elaborated with a shrubbery to the west and formal grass terraces on the east side, where the front of the dairy built in *c.*1846 formed a decorative feature. A layout of rose beds was contrived before the south front. There was also a rustic pergola, a rustic wooden bridge over the lake, and a boat house on its banks. These features have all disappeared, and the garden has been continuously remodelled in this century, but the stone Tuscan temple of *c.*1846, the front of the dairy when first built, survives but re-sited. Alan Good regraded the lawns round the house and built the stone terraces on the south front (using material from the demolished back parts of the house) as well as extending the ha-ha to the west as part of his alterations in the late 1940s.

Looking from the Family Games Room to the East Garden.

The great storm in 1987 caused a lot of damage to the park, blowing down many of the older trees. Alan Bond during his brief ownership made drastic alterations, notably the widening of the lake and the construction of an island on it. By 1990 the park and garden had lost much of their clarity and interest. New tree planting had been carried on without any regard to the contours or the historical layout, all the greenhouses in the walled garden had been demolished, and mown grass and shrubbery extended from the garden into the park proper, where extensive planting of conifers had added a further incongruous note into the arcadian, pastoral landscape.

A major part of the improvement programme for Glympton has been the restoration of the park landscape and redesign of the garden. A master-plan was commissioned in 1991 from the well-known garden designer, François Goffinet, and many of his recommendations have been carried into effect, though it will be some years before all the new planting has fully matured. The aim has been to devise an overall treatment for the landscape, rather than piecemeal adaptation of individual areas. The master plan was based on historical research and site and tree surveys. Goffinet's principal recommendations were the restoration of the Glyme to the old dimensions, shown in the 1881 Ordnance Survey map, the establishment of a belt walk in the 18th-century tradition round the edge of the park to give changing views, and the redesign of the park planting to reflect more closely its historic character.

In the garden the aim has been to simplify and define the surroundings of the house and to restore the historic balance between immediate garden formality and more distant landscape informality. A new forecourt and carriage sweep have been created on the west side.

The 1846 entrance porch reconstructed in the East Garden as a pavilion.

Inside the new boathouse.

To the south, Good's post-war stone-paved terraces have been retained, but the lawn simplified and the ha-ha retained on its 18th-century lines. East of the house two formal gardens—a terrace garden and a sunken garden—have been created in conjunction with the part subterranean building extensions on that side of the house. The 1846 Tuscan portico, removed from the west front to make way for the new porte-cochère, has been re-erected on this side as a free-standing temple. The Dairy pavilion has been moved and is now sited overlooking the lower lawn from the north end. A new timber boat house with decorative open-work barge-boards has also been erected beside the lake according to the proposal made by François Goffinet. These alterations have successfully transformed the surroundings of the house, which now comprise clearly defined formal gardens while the eye is led into the landscape beyond by means of a series of well-sited new decorative structures.

Future proposals for the embellishment of the park include the construction of a thatched rustic pavilion beside the lake, a grotto, and the possible extension of the lake into the North Park which at the moment is featureless. It is also proposed to restore the walled garden as a private garden for the use of the owner and his guests. Although improvements will continue for many years, Glympton has already recaptured its 18th-century spirit; the park is lightly grazed by sheep, and new planting of trees and shrubs now leads the eye along the sinuous line of the restored Glyme. From the belt drive, picturesque views can be obtained of the house in its redesigned setting, of South Lodge on its eminence and, over the lake, to the other restored landscape features. Once more Glympton presents a coherently designed landscape as intended by its creators in the 17th and 18th centuries.

The new boathouse on the river Glyme.

v — The Parish Church

The church was originally dedicated to St Lawrence but by the early 18th century the name had been changed to St Mary, though the parish feast was still held on or near St Lawrence's day. The exact date of the church's foundation is not known. It was already in existence at the beginning of the 12th century and is mentioned in a deed of gift dating from between 1101 and 1110. Geoffrey de Clinton gave the rectory to his new priory at Kenilworth in 1122. The oldest parts of the existing structure date from the 12th century.

Though much rebuilt and restored over the centuries, the church keeps its original simple Norman form of a four-bay nave, without aisles, and a three-bay chancel. The present tower probably dates from the 16th century but incorporates fragments of re-used Norman masonry including bits of carved zig zag or chevron. The tower arch and chancel arch, the latter with dog tooth ornament, are both fine Norman features (though the chancel arch was widened and restored in the 19th century). The simple stone font also dates from the 12th century.

The nave was remodelled in the 1730s, when round-arched windows were inserted and a classical pediment was added to the south doorway. The outer walls with sturdy buttresses survive, however, and are medieval. The church was repaired in about 1850, after the Barnetts inherited the estate. But the major Victorian restoration was undertaken in 1872 when the Revd C.M. Bartholomew was the energetic rector and Frank Henry Barnett, a keen churchman, had inherited the estate. The architect was G.E. Street, the surveyor to the Oxford diocese. Street was one of the leading Victorian Gothic Revival architects, responsible for the new Law Courts in London and many new and restored Anglican churches throughout the country.

The Norman parish church; the tower is early 16th century.

He virtually rebuilt the chancel and replaced the Georgian windows in the nave with new pointed ones in decorated 14th-century style and erected a new hammerbeam roof. He also added the well-designed south porch and the vestry. It is thanks to Street's restoration that the church today seems such an undisturbed example of an ancient church. The old font is reputed to have been found at that time in the village being used as a watering trough and was reinstated in the church as part of the 1872 works. On the inside of the north pier of the chancel arch is a rare but incomplete Latin inscription dating from the 12th century and no doubt recording the original building. It reads *'Dedicatio Huius Templi Idus Martii …'* [This church was dedicated on 15 March …].

The interior is light and pleasant with lime-washed walls. There are a number of family monuments to successive squires of Glympton, including a late-Georgian Neo-classical marble tablet to Francis Sackville Lloyd Wheate, only son of Richard Lloyd and Mary, co-heiress of Sir Thomas Wheate Bt. He died in 1812. Inset into the paved floor of the nave are a series of black ledger stones commemorating successive members of the Wheate family: Thomas Wheate (died 1668); Frances Wheate his wife (died 1706); Sir Thomas Wheate Bt (1721); Sir Thomas Wheate Bt (1746) and Sir George Wheate Bt (1751). In the churchyard is a stone cross erected in 1897 in memory of Henry Barnett (died 1896). There is also a memorial tablet for Alan Good.

The principal monument is, however, that to the Tesdales in the chancel. It was erected in 1616 under the terms of the will of Maud Tesdale and is a fine piece of Jacobean carving in alabaster with kneeling figures of Thomas Tesdale and his wife Maud. It was repaired in 1704 by Pembroke College, Oxford, who regard him as their co-founder. On the monument itself and on adjoining

The Norman font.

The Tesdale Monument erected in 1616.

Interior of the church with Norman chancel arch and Victorian roof.

marble and brass panels is a series of Latin and English inscriptions, epitaphs and verses. They read as follows:

Latin inscription over the man's head:

EX QUO TANDEM

HUC UBI NESTOREOS IMPLERUNT STAMINA SOLES

HUMANA IN FOVEAM DEJUCIT OSSA LIGO

INDISTINCTA PATET CALVARIA NEC MINUS URGET

ORA SUPER REGES QUAM SUPER ORA GREGIS

[Since here
when the thread of life had equalled Nestor's years,
the spade into the pit the bones of man did cast,
the skull without distinction lies; nor is the weight
less on the bones of kings than on the bones of
common folk.]

Latin inscription over the woman's head:

DISCE MORI

MAXIMA NOSSE MORI VITAE EST SAPIENTIA VIVIT

QUI MORITUR SI VIS VIVERE DISCE MORI

VITA PRIOR MORTEM SED MORS TIBI PRIMA
SECUNDAM

VITAM QUAE VITA EST NON MORITURA DABIR

[The Lesson of Death
The chief wisdom of life is knowledge how to
die.
He lives who dies. If thou wilt live, learn how to
die.
Life first brings death, but death it is that first
Bestows a second life that never death shall know.]

Latin inscription on the central panel:

HOC FUNDATORIS SUI MONUMENTUM PENE

COLLAPSUM INSTAURARUNT MAGISTER ET SOCH

COLL. PEMBROCHIANI OXON A.D. 1704.

[This monument of their Founder
When near to ruin, was restored
By the Master and Fellows
Of Pembroke College Oxon A.D. 1704]

Latin verse, hexameter and pentameter, at the foot of MAUD TESDALE'S Inscription:

SIC SIC CAELESTIS QUI LUX ES SINGULA LUSTRANS

VIVERE DA NOBIS DA BENE CHRISTE MORI

[Do Thou, the Light of Heaven,—that shines on
all,
Grant us so to live; grant well, O Christ, to die.]

Latin Maxims at the two bottom corners of the Monument:

TERRENA VIDE CABLESTIA CREDE

[What is earthly, thou seest; what is heavenly,
believe.]

PIETAS IN FINE CORONAT

[A crown rewards a godly life.]

White Swan House, once the village inn, and restored stocks.

There are five church bells dating from the 18th and 19th centuries, one dated 1784, and a sanctus of 1705. The 19th-century ones were given by the Barnett family.

The church plate includes a pewter alms-dish and flagon reputed to have been stolen by Cromwell's soldiers in the Civil War and which were recovered in London three hundred years later and presented by Alan Good.

Rectors of St Mary's Church, Glympton, Oxfordshire, 1237-1992
Diocese of Lincoln

1237	Master Alexander de Langeford	1578	William Woodwarde
	Patrons—The Prior and Convent of Kenilworth	1620	George Woodwarde
1245	Walter de Ravenesden	1655	Nathaniell Staniforthe
	Robert *called* Schirlock *died* 1291	1662	John Robinson—Patron—Thomas Wheate
1291	Nicholas de Saltford	1684	Stephen Penton—Patron—Frances Wheate
1294	Ralph de Salle	1693	John Hacker, MA—Patron—Frances Wheate
1305	John de Lenton	1732	Samuel Jones, MA—Patron—Sir Thomas Wheate
1309	John de Salle	1741	George Huddesford, DD
1337	Thomas de Bannebury	1776	Sir Henry Parker, Barr
1355	Sir Thomas Preest	1782	William Flamank, MA
1381	John Lye	1795	William Flamank, DD
1394	Sir David Roberde	1818	Thomas Nucella
	Philip Wayte—died 1406	1856	Charles Bartholomew—Patron—George Barnett Esq
1406	Sir Hugh Olyf	1897	William Groves, MA—Patron—Frank Barnett Esq
	Thomas Rouke—resigned 1454	1908	Gother Mann—Patron—George Barnett Esq
1454	Sir John Clyffird	1909	Arthur Wilson
1461	Sir Hugh Runton	1912	Herbert Sawyer, MA
1466	Sir Henry Hoghton	1923	John Erskine Bowles
1470	Sir Geoffrey Bardyzay	1933	Charles Henry Cox, BSc
1501	Sir Fulk Salisbury	1961	Arthur Charles Cox
Diocese of Oxford		1970	Gordon Wilkins
	(George Gelybrand—died 1546)	1974	Cecil du Heoume
1546	Edward Gabet—Patrons—The Crown	1980	R.G. Mulrenan—Patron—E.W. Towler
1558	Richard Griffith—Patron—J. Cupper—Gent	1981	John Sergeant—Patron—E.W. Towler
1559	William Owsley	1990	Leonard Doolan—Patron—New College, Oxford
1568	John Raynforth	1992	Robert Farman—Patron—New College, Oxford

The village street showing the former school (right) and the Post Office (centre).

Almshouses designed by Trenwith Wills in 1949 for Alan Good.

Detail of carved stone cartouche on the almshouses.

VI — The Village and Rectory

The village was originally situated next to the church on a scarp within an elbow of the River Glyme, which provided an ideal situation for a settlement. The occupation of this site was extremely ancient. An excavation of the area to the north west of the church in 1994 by the Oxford Archaeological Unit revealed not just some plot boundary walls of part of the cleared medieval village but evidence of Iron-Age occupation in the area including six circular pits, and sherds of Middle and Late Iron-Age pottery and part of a stone axe head. The presence of Roman pottery suggests that the site was occupied from the Iron Age into Roman times.

It seems likely that the centre of the medieval village was to the west of the church where the walled garden is now. It has been suggested that the asymmetrical shape of the walled garden may have been based on a vanished feature of the old village, such as the village green. The church, and probably the house, are the only buildings now to remain on their medieval sites. The rest of the village was cleared away in the 1630s and 1640s by William Wheate at the time he enclosed the park.

He moved the village to the south east, beside the River Glyme and the road from Wootton to Enstone, which in the 17th century formed part of the main road from London to Aberystwyth. It, and its branch to Woodstock later part of the main road from Oxford to

Stratford and the Midlands, was turnpiked in 1729 and remained a turnpike till 1878. The London road brought prosperity to the village inn, *The White Swan*, which closed in 1853 and is now a private house called White Swan House. From the 19th century onwards most traffic used the Oxford-Woodstock-Chipping Norton road, further to the south, and Glympton became a quiet backwater. It was otherwise in the past. In the 17th century the village complained that it was 'much charged and burdened with cripples, poor passengers and vagrants' passing through. This is supported by the parish registers which record the burial of several pauper travellers.

The former inn is, apart from the rectory, the oldest building in the village. It is a substantial L-shaped house of two storeys and attics, built of coursed rubble stone. It is now of 18th-century date. But an alehouse at Glympton is recorded in 1648. By the end of the 17th century it was a large and well-equipped establishment, with 13 rooms. The will of the inn-keeper who died in 1699 recorded goods worth £563, including 21 bedsteads, 40 pairs of sheets, 35 pewter dishes, five dozen plates, 78 napkins and 19 table cloths.

Like all the rest of the village, White Swan House belongs to the estate. It was occupied after 1878 by the manager of the Home Farm.

The majority of the cottages in the village now date from the 19th century and were built by successive Barnett squires. The number of cottages in the village rose from about six in the 17th century to 10 in 1811 and to 34 in 1861. The last surviving 18th-century cottages are Blacks Cottages on the Wootton road, a semi-detached pair of rubble stone, with stone slated roofs, and ancient windows with leaded panes. They are listed Grade II. Glyme Cottages facing the river and rectory garden were built by G.H. Barnett in about 1850, and are characteristic Victorian model cottages with canopied porches over the doors. The Post Office was established in 1887, according to Kelly's *Directories*. The former school, further to the north, is a more ornamental structure, given a slight Gothic feel by steep gables with barge-boards, and a projecting porch. It was built in 1849 by G.H. Barnett, soon after he inherited the estate, and remained in use till 1932. It is now the parish hall and social centre of the village, having been converted by Alan Good for that purpose in 1950.

After the Second World War Alan Good greatly improved the village and built several new houses in the late 1940s. These comprise the six semi-detached cottages along New Road on the edge of the playing field to the east of the village. Like their Victorian predecessors

General view of the village street in 1998.

they are constructed of local stone in the Cotswold tradition. He also built and endowed the almshouses next to the Village Hall in 1949 as a memorial to his daughter who died young. They contain accommodation for four elderly people. They were designed by Trenwith Wills and are an elegant exercise in the local vernacular with steep stone-flagged roofs, tall square chimneystacks, mullion windows and an elaborate carved cartouche, containing the date and dedication, in the central gable. They were built of local stone, and show the influence of early 20th-century Arts and Crafts architects like Sir Edwin Lutyens and Detmar Blow. This is not surprising as Wills had been taught architecture by Lutyens at the Royal Academy Schools and had worked for Detmar Blow as a young man. Each unit comprised a living room and a bedroom, divided from each other by a curtained opening so that anyone 'confined to bed could entertain friends and enjoy the warmth of the up to date grate'. There was also a modern kitchen and bathroom in each. They were published in *Country Life* in 1954.

Much repair and restoration of the buildings in the village has been carried out by the present owner since 1991. The old village stocks have been restored to their original position in the middle of the village, by the side of the river, having been moved to the churchyard in the 1950s. Much of its attraction comes from the homogeneous use of local building materials including stone slates on the roofs, and the layout of the buildings beside the River Glyme, the course of which was altered in the 18th century and converted to its present appearance as a wide shallow stream, with little waterfalls in the rectory garden. The Georgian stone bridge over the river may have been built at the time of the diversion. It is first mentioned in 1797 and was repaired by the County in 1842.

The old Rectory was bought by the estate in 1995 and is to be refurbished to provide a secondary house for the owner's family. The new work and refurbishment is being designed by Nicholas Johnston and Peter Cave who have been architects for many of the recent improvements at Glympton. It formerly belonged to the Oxford Diocese but was sold off in 1961 and became a private house at that date. It is a spacious but plain stone-built Georgian house. Over the front door is an old fire insurance mark, with a portcullis and Prince of Wales feathers, for the Westminster Fire Office. (In the 18th century, the insurance companies paid for the fire engines which didn't turn out for a fire unless the building was insured by them, hence the prominent display of the insurance company's mark on front elevations.)

The Georgian stone bridge over the river Glyme.

The medieval rectory at Glympton was sited next to the church in what is now Glympton park. It was taxed on eight hearths in 1665 and was described as being a seven-bay building in 1685. It seems likely that it was given up shortly afterwards and that the rectory was moved to the present site in the village in c.1690. The glebe was consolidated and enclosed in the 1690s. Also in 1690 it was recorded that 'dilapidated buildings' at the old rectory were demolished and rebuilt 'in a more convenient place'. The oldest part of the present house (the kitchen) dates from about that time.

The move to the existing site followed the moving of the village in the 1630s and 1640s. The rector obviously followed his flock 50 years afterwards.

The rectory as it is today is the product of a series of alterations and additions. The original late 17th-century building was probably only one room deep, corresponding to the back half (including the kitchen) of the existing house; that part of the building still has thicker walls and more irregular rooms than the front of the house. Traces of the original long, low windows with wooden lintels can still be seen in the back elevation. The building assumed its present double-pile plan in the 18th century. It is shown in this form on Jeffery's *Oxon Map* (1767) and also in a map of 1807 by 'Mr Pratley of the parish' (used for the 1837 Glympton tithe award). Some work was done to the grounds in 1788 when the River Glyme was diverted as part of the rector's 'improvements' and made more ornamental. The principal remodelling of the house, however, seems to have taken place between 1803 and 1805. All the interesting internal details of the house (apart from some earlier 18th-century two-panel doors) date from this phase, including the double-hung sashes with thin glazing bars in the windows of the principal rooms, the simple but elegant staircase with its slightly gothick tread ends, and several of the chimneypieces, with reeded surrounds and cast-iron grates.

The east wing, containing a study on the ground floor and bedroom above, was built in 1887 for the then rector, the Revd C.M. Bartholomew (rector of Glympton from 1856 to 1897). No architect is recorded for this extension, which, apart from a few gothic touches, keeps to the plain Georgian vernacular style of the main house; it is probable that it was the work of a local builder to the rector's instructions and that no architect was employed. The glazed front porch was no doubt added by Mr. Bartholomew at almost the same time.

The old Rectory.

The Glympton pedigree herd of Aberdeen Angus cattle.

VII — *The Estate Farms*

The estate today comprises 2,510 acres all farmed in hand with a resident farm manager. The crops are not that different from William Wheate's in the 17th century: including wheat, barley and peas. There is also a flock of breeding ewes, which echo the sheep and cattle raising enterprises of earlier times, and a herd of Aberdeen Angus cattle. Although intensively farmed, the estate has several areas of woodland and a well known Cotswold 'Site of Special Scientific Interest' at Sheep's Bank with rich wild flower grassland and an ancient hedge.

Substantial works of landscape restoration and improvement have been undertaken since 1991. Many miles of new predominantly hawthorn hedge have been planted to restore this traditional landscape feature which contributes so much to the visual appeal of the English countryside and provides an irreplaceable habitat for wild life. Many new trees have also been planted, both in hedgerows and in small coverts, the latter partly to provide for the pheasant shoot which has been established and developed since 1991. The woods now comprise two hundred acres of established woodland, principally at Glympton Heath and at Assart. One hundred and seventy acres of mixed broadleaf young plantations have been planted since 1988.

Large and ugly modern, industrial-style farm buildings erected by Eric Towler in the 1960s and 1970s have all been demolished. At Home Farm, to the north of the village, the old buildings have been restored and rebuilt in the traditional manner using local stone and other vernacular materials. The new buildings there were designed by the Agricultural Development and Advisory Service. Some of the old buildings here have been ingeniously adapted to serve as the estate office with the original beamed roof visible in the Meeting Room upstairs.

New hedge planting on the estate.

New farm buildings at Home Farm.

Inside the new farm buildings.

At Hill Farm, to the south of the village, ugly modern buildings have all been removed and the old buildings which were in poor condition have been restored and converted to a shooting lodge. They comprise a farmhouse, former stables, granary and barn all dating from *c.*1800. They are listed Grade II and all built of coursed local stone. All these were in very ramshackle condition and the house was latterly lived in by the estate shepherd. They were restored in 1992 by the estate. The barn is now a splendid dining room for shoot lunches. The former pig sties have been rebuilt as the kitchen. The interior has been designed by Joanna Wood in a robust simple fashion well-suited to its function.

The oldest and most interesting historic farm building on the estate is Ludwell. This is now the house of the resident estate manager. It dates from the 16th century and is listed Grade II. It was originally a separate manor, in the parish of Wootton. At the time of the Domesday Survey in 1086 there were five estates in Ludwell, of which this one was owned by Ranulph. Later it was held, not by military service, but by serjeancy of tending the royal garden at Woodstock Manor. The village itself was wiped out in the Black Death. Later, in the 18th and 19th centuries it belonged to the Dashwood estate at Kirtlington; it has only been added to the Glympton estate in this century. The land there was bought by Eric Towler in 1958, but the house was sold and only bought back again in 1992. It is built of stone with stone mullioned and pointed arch windows and is a substantial structure. It was described as a 'mansion house' in 1571. The main range once comprised a full height hall, parlour and screens passage. On the first floor were two chambers, one with an arch-braced roof, and closet. The staircase, kitchens and service room were on the east side, but this wing was rebuilt in 1879, incorporating some old walling. The house retains much original oak panelling and several moulded stone fireplaces.

There are several scheduled ancient monuments on the estate, evidence of man's occupation of this part of Oxfordshire for four thousand years. Copping Knoll is a Bronze-Age bowl barrow thought to date from around 2,000 BC. It is a prominent local feature. The most important monuments, however, are three sections of Grims Ditch that run through the estate at Assarts Farm on the west side of the Woodstock-Chipping Norton road. They are part of an extensive Iron-Age system of linear earthworks which is thought originally to have formed a protective rampart round the farm and settled land in the pre-Roman north Oxfordshire uplands, which were otherwise heavily wooded in prehistoric times. Grims Ditch is the largest sub-circular enclosure in the British Isles of any period and is therefore a monument of considerable importance.

Inside the barn at Hill Farm now used for shooting lunches.

Hill Farm restored and converted to the shooting lodge in 1992.

Ludwell House. It dates from the 16th century and is now the residence of the agent.

The estate land is divided as follows. There are 1,420 acres of arable, 280 acres of permanent pasture, 136 acres of improved pasture and 375 acres of woodland. The farms which make up the estate today have been acquired at different times. At the centre of the estate is Home Farm. The estate office is situated here, and all farming operations are now conducted from here. The complex of buildings includes a grain store with a capacity of 3,400 tonnes, two large livestock units for in-wintering of cattle and sheep, and associated stone-built workshops and storage buildings. To the north is Heath Farm which was first reclaimed for arable farming by William Wheate in the 17th century. To the west is Rectory Farm, once known as Glebe Farm and which historically provided the income for the rector's stipend. It was bought from the Church of England in the 1920s by George Henry Barnett. In the east Ludwell Farm was, as has been seen, part of the Dashwood's Kirtlington estate and was bought by Eric Towler in the 1950s. In the south east Balliol Farm was at one time part of the Duke of Marlborough's Blenheim estate but had been sold off, and was added to Glympton in the mid-1990s. Manor Farm is situated to the east of the Wootton-Glympton boundary and has been slowly incorporated into the Glympton estate over many years, two further land purchases in this area having taken place in the 1990s. (The former farm-house and two fields are still in separate ownership.) Hill Farm, south of the village, is the shooting lodge. Assarts Farm on the south boundary was reclaimed from the Forest of Wychwood in the Middle Ages and has formed part of the Glympton estate since that time, though some land there has been sold at various dates, most recently by Eric Towler. Assart is a medieval word meaning clearing in a forest for arable farming (derived from French). So the modern name perpetuates the origins of this area.

The farm today comprises two thirds winter-sown crops and one third spring-sown crops. High quality crops are grown: malting and feed barley (the former for beer, the latter for farm animals), milling and feed wheat (the former for bread), peas, linseed and oilseed rape (the latter two being modern crops which would not have been known to the Wheates). The farm is geared to catering for niche markets, this being a relatively reliable means of obtaining full value for crops. The farm also maintains a commercial flock of 600 breeding ewes who produce over 1,100 lambs each year. In addition 180 ewe lambs are purchased each autumn and those not required for incorporation into the breeding flock are sold as gimmers (Viking for a ewe between her first and second shearing) the following year. An Aberdeen Angus pedigree herd of cattle was established in 1993 and now comprises 40 cows. It is intended to expand this slowly to a maximum of 50 cows. Altogether, Glympton is an excellent example of how a traditional landed estate can be developed to preserve and enhance the landscape while being efficiently farmed to produce high grade crops for specialist markets.